MW01076319

Making It Through the Middle

Making It Through the Middle

Hope and Help When the Journey Seems Long

EMILY FREEMAN

DESERET
BOOK

Salt Lake City, Utah

© 2014 Emily Freeman

All rights reserved. No part of this book may be reproduced in any form or by any means without permission in writing from the publisher, Deseret Book Company, at permissions@deseretbook.com or P. O. Box 30178, Salt Lake City, Utah 84130. This work is not an official publication of The Church of Jesus Christ of Latter-day Saints. The views expressed herein are the responsibility of the author and do not necessarily represent the position of the Church or of Deseret Book Company.

Deseret Book is a registered trademark of Deseret Book Company.

Visit us at DeseretBook.com

Library of Congress Cataloging-in-Publication Data
CIP data on file
ISBN 978-1-60907-822-5

Printed in the United States of America
R. R. Donnelley, Crawfordsville, IN

10 9 8 7 6 5 4 3 2 1

For Heath and Steph
Something good will come of this

Do not question too much, dear friend,
For the God who ordained the beginning
Can safely be trusted with the end,
As well as with all that lies between.

Myrtle Reed

Middle Moments

Do you have a bucket list?

I do.

It's a list of things I have always wanted to do. Sometimes it takes me a little while to check something off my list. For example, in a small town right by where I live, they put on a live nativity every year. I have wanted to go for almost a decade, ever since we moved here. Last year we finally went, and I invited my brother and his family to come with us.

Everyone in the whole world must have decided to check that experience off their bucket list that night. The line to get in to the nativity was so long! It was dark and cold, and we couldn't even see the entrance from our place in the line. After we had been there for almost an hour, my seven-year-old nephew, Mack, finally looked up at his dad and said, "It's worth it to give up."

We laughed and laughed at his simple solution. But we didn't give up. We waited. Then, finally, we were there. We saw kings who followed a star, shepherds who bore testimony, and at the finish we entered a hushed stable and found the Lord. In the end, it wasn't "worth it to give up" after all.

Have you ever had a time in your life that found you wanting to express the sentiment of my nephew because you were so tired of waiting for the end to come?

Perhaps you have waited too long for an answer. Maybe your heart is aching with unrest. You might feel like you have forgotten what it is like to feel joy.

When we are in the middle of a challenge, it is hard for us to picture what lies ahead. It can be particularly hard to imagine the goodness that is waiting there. Often, in the middle of that hard place, we wonder how much longer it will last and how we will ever make it through.

I don't know how this book ended up in your hands, but hopefully the message contained within these pages is just what you need right now. I pray these words will allow the Spirit to touch your heart and lead you in the direction you need to travel. Might I offer a word of encouragement? If you wonder if waiting for the answer, the promise, or the miracle is worth it . . . it is.

> *"Behold, the days come, saith the Lord,*
> *that I will perform that good thing*
> *which I have promised."*
> *Jeremiah 33:14*

Don't give up.

Not only will you make it through this, there are good things to come.

Such is the promise of the Lord.

1

Journeys

Have you ever noticed that when people talk about their trials in a public setting, they tend to focus on what happened at the end? They talk about the miracle, the promise, the way it all worked out. It isn't often that people talk about what happened in the middle of the trial.

So what happens if you are in the middle?

What if the promise, or the miracle, or the answer you long for is nowhere in sight? Have you ever wondered where you might go to find the answers that will help you get through the middle moments of your life?

The scriptures are filled with accounts of journeys. Moses, Joshua, Abraham, Noah, Jeremiah, Lehi, Nephi, and Jared are just a few who had to make a journey of some kind. If you go back and read through their records carefully; you will realize there is more recorded in their histories than just their arrival at the promised land. The whole journey has been captured in writing—even the moments of waiting that happened in the middle.

If you are looking for answers, these scriptural accounts are one of the best places you can turn. Don't read what happened at the end of the journey; instead focus on the chapters that talk about the moments in the middle. What counsel does the Lord give in those chapters? What questions does He ask? What promises does He covenant to keep? Then spend some time considering how the people in those chapters responded to His counsel. What action was required on their part? What did they learn and experience?

> **Middle Moments**
> **Recorded in the Scriptures**
> Genesis 6
> Exodus 13, 16, 33
> Deuteronomy 2, 6, 7
> Joshua 2, 3
> Jeremiah 26, 29, 31
> 1 Nephi 17–18
> Ether 2, 3, 6

The nuggets of counsel, inspired questions, and certain promises from the Lord found in the scriptures can help guide us through the middle moments of our own lives. Within the pages of this book you will discover some of these journeys. A sincere search through the standard works will lead you to discover even more journeys that you can study and learn from.

Remember, just as every journey has a beginning and an end, it also has a middle.

You will make it through this one.

The Lord will show you how.

LESSON ONE

Turn to the Scriptures

2

Every Day Better

One August afternoon we were invited to go boating with our neighbors. They gave us thirty minutes to get ready and jump into the car. There wasn't a second to spare—it wouldn't be long before the late afternoon would become evening and the late-summer sun would be gone.

In no time we were driving down the street behind our neighbors. Within ten minutes we had turned onto the lane that led to the harbor. We were making great time, and anticipation for one last summer hoorah filled the conversation with excitement. And then my daughter Megan groaned, "Oh no! The road's closed! This is the only way into the harbor! Mom! What are we going to do?"

We all stared at the Road Closed sign in front of

us, the anticipation quickly evaporating out of the car. This road really was the only way we knew to get to the harbor. After a moment's pause, our friends drove around the sign and down the lane. My kids cheered as I followed behind. The enthusiasm was short-lived, however. It wasn't long before we found ourselves stopped in front of a gaping hole with a huge tractor in front. There was no way past.

"I guess we're not going," I said.

"What about the detour signs?" my son Caleb asked. I remembered the signs that had been posted above the Road Closed sign.

"I just don't think those signs will lead to the harbor," I replied.

Caleb immediately responded, "Mom, if there's a detour sign, then that means there really is a way through."

I had never thought of a detour sign in that way before. For me, that detour sign represented a dead end, a change of plans, an unexpected route that would take longer if indeed it would get me to my destination at all.

To him, the sign represented hope—a way through.

He was right.

We followed the carefully placed signs until we reached the harbor. It took a little longer, and it was definitely unexpected, but we made it through the road closure and spent a wonderful evening making memories with our friends.

In the book of Joshua, we read of a group of people whose journey was stopped short because of a huge obstacle. In a scene reminiscent of crossing the Red Sea, Joshua and the children of Israel were cut off at the banks of the Jordan River. A detour, or a way through, would have to be provided. So Joshua turned to the Lord.

You might remember when the river parted and stood "upon an heap" (Joshua 3:13, 16) so the people of Israel could cross through. That miracle is found at the very end of Joshua 3. But have you ever taken the time to study the first part of Joshua 3? It is the middle moment of that great journey.

As Joshua stood looking at the obstacle ahead, the Lord gave him the counsel he would need to proceed: "When ye see the ark of the covenant of the Lord your God . . . *go after it* . . . that ye may know the way by which ye must go: *for ye have not passed this way heretofore*" (Joshua 3:3–4; emphasis added). The ark became like the detour signs—a means to help Israel through.

Have you ever come to a point in a trial where you didn't know what to do? How to proceed? What direction to take? The Lord counseled Joshua to go after the ark so he would know the way to go, *because he had not passed that way heretofore*. There will be moments in our own lives when we will not know how to proceed. The Lord has given us sources of direction and places where we can go to receive revelation for those times. The scriptures, Church meetings, and temple worship are a few of the sources of this inspiration. But we have to *go after it*. We have to put forth the effort. Action on our part will be required.

Then the Lord gave Joshua a wonderful promise, "Sanctify yourselves: *for to morrow the Lord will do wonders among you*" (Joshua 3:5; emphasis added). I love to imagine Joshua standing before the Jordan River on the evening before that great miracle took place. What thoughts filled his mind as he looked at that huge obstacle, which was swollen to flooding over its banks? Did he wonder how his people would ever get through? Was it hard to sleep that night? Did the waiting for the wonder that was about to take place weigh upon his mind?

I wonder if he wished they could overcome the obstacle that instant. Was it hard when the Lord said it would have to wait until tomorrow?

Sometimes we experience trials that stop us in our tracks. We become as Joshua—we stand at the banks of the great obstacle and wait for the inspiration that will help us get through. Sometimes the detour takes us on a route we don't anticipate. Sometimes the promise doesn't come until tomorrow. But one thing is certain—the Lord will lead us through. Our tomorrows will come.

This past winter I experienced an illness that knocked me off my feet. It is the sickest I have ever been. I was down in bed for almost four months, and although I visited doctor after doctor, no one could find a solution. Finally, after several prayers, priesthood blessings, and tender mercies, I found a doctor who could help. He warned me that the progress would be slow.

I am not a patient person, and the waiting to get better was excruciating. My aunt called one day to encourage me. As we finished the conversation, she reminded me, "This isn't the twenty-four-hour flu; you could have months of recovery ahead." It was the first time in my life I have actually wanted to have the twenty-four-hour flu.

I spent most afternoons in tears, and finally one day I called a good friend for counsel. I poured out my heart to him and then asked for advice. He replied,

"The problem is that you are looking at the peak. You need to be looking at the pickup truck."

"What are you talking about?" I asked incredulously.

So he explained. "Pretend you are on a hike. You are spending so much time looking at the peak, at where you want to be, that you can't see how far you have come. Turn around every so often and look back at the pickup truck where you left it in the parking lot."

I realized I needed to stop and take note of how far I had come, how much I had grown. I needed to recognize that the Lord was moving me toward the promise even if the progress was taking longer than I thought it should.

My friend's advice prepared me for a tender mercy the Lord would send a few days later. Knowing that my life had taken an unanticipated detour, I turned to the scriptures. In the book of Mosiah I stumbled upon a scripture that reminded me of our conversation: "And it came to pass that they began to *prosper by degrees* in the land" (Mosiah 21:16; emphasis added). I read of people who were in bondage, who carried heavy burdens, who were in the middle of a moment of great affliction. Several chapters later there was a verse that said, "And it came to pass that so great was their faith and their patience that the voice of the Lord came unto them again, saying: Be of good comfort, for *on the morrow* I will deliver you out of bondage" (Mosiah 24:16; emphasis added).

Because I had been prepared, I didn't miss the two phrases *prosper by degrees* and *on the morrow*. I typed up the verses and hung them in my room where I would see them every morning right when I woke up. At the top of the paper I wrote one phrase: *Every Day Better*.

Every Day Better

Prosper by Degrees

On the Morrow

Part of mortality includes detours along the way, storms that slow us down, and obstacles that must be surmounted. When we encounter those things, we have to learn to wait on the Lord and to realize that His wonders might not come until tomorrow. We must also remember that sometimes the miracle doesn't come all at once—sometimes it comes by degrees. Through this process we learn patience, we learn submission, we learn humility, and we become sanctified.

If it ever feels like you have waited so long that you aren't moving forward anymore, if you feel like you have taken an unexpected detour, if you wonder if your tomorrow will ever come . . . stop and look back at the truck. Then go after the Lord's revelation. Remember that sometimes it won't be until tomorrow that the Lord will do wonders among us, but His wonders will come.

He will provide a way through.

Keep in mind that the miracle you seek may not be discernible from the middle of the journey. In fact, you might not discover it until you have exhausted every effort and followed every detour. Then, suddenly, one day it will be there. You should know that it will be magnificent. Remarkable. And in that moment you will stand still in wonder and admire the greatness of God.

It will be worth the detour it takes to get there.

Of this, I am certain.

LESSON TWO

Wait Patiently; Tomorrow Will Come

Grace Shall Be as Your Day

Come, come, ye Saints, no toil nor labor fear;
But with joy wend your way.
Though hard to you this journey may appear,
Grace shall be as your day.
("Come, Come, Ye Saints," Hymns, no. 30)

If you could choose a soundtrack for the epic journeys of the Lord's people, this song would surely top the list. It is filled with advice for the weary traveler. As I was singing this song recently, the last line of the stanza above stood out to me: *Grace shall be as your day.* I have pondered the meaning of that line many times, but suddenly it became clear to me—the grace, or enabling and strengthening power, we desire will be given according to the needs of our day. In other words, "Grace will be given as your day requires."

Another favorite hymn teaches this same principle: "As thy days may demand, so thy succor shall be" ("How Firm a Foundation," *Hymns,* no. 85).

The story of the children of Israel receiving manna from heaven teaches this principle. After wandering in the wilderness for several days, the people began to get hungry. They approached Moses with their worry, and he approached the Lord. The Lord poured out blessings from heaven upon them. Literally. "Behold, I will rain bread from heaven for you; . . . in the morning bread to the full; . . . and ye shall know that I am the Lord your God" (Exodus 16:4, 8, 12). His grace was sent to fill their need every day for the next forty years. Do you ever wonder if the same principle is true for us today?

I believe in a God who continually ministers to His people. One of the definitions of the word *minister* is "to tend to." The Lord tends to us with mercy. Consider those two ideas together and you come up with a phrase that is familiar to us—*tender mercy.* I believe it is the personal ministering of His mercy that makes those moments so tender. A friend told me that in Finnish the phrase *tender mercies* is written *lempeät armoteot,* which translates directly as "gentle works of grace." I love that translation. The Lord is tender and gentle in His ministry to us. Just as the children of Israel experienced blessings from heaven daily during their middle moments, we can too. Theirs came in the form of manna; ours come in the form of tender mercies.

The Lord set forth the rules of the manna: "And the children of Israel . . . gathered, some more, some less . . . every man according to his eating" (Exodus 16:17–18). The people were told to gather only as much as they needed, but no extra because the extra would not last through the night. What would fill and nourish them had to be gathered every day except the Sabbath. Perhaps the same is true of us today. Somehow we must learn to recognize the tender mercies of the Lord in our lives every single day. Storing them up will not work.

Elder David A. Bednar defined tender mercies as

"very personal and individualized blessings, strength, protection, assurances, guidance, loving-kindnesses, consolation, support, and spiritual gifts which we receive from and because of and through the Lord Jesus Christ" ("Tender Mercies," 99). Consider Elder Bednar's list. How long has it been since you have recognized a tender mercy that fits that definition? Do you recognize the hand of the Lord in your life daily? Do you recognize some more, some less, according to your need?

At the end of the chapter written about the manna, the Lord told Moses, "Fill an omer of it to be kept for your generations; that they may see the bread wherewith I have fed you in the wilderness, . . . so Aaron laid it up before the Testimony, to be kept" (Exodus 16:32–34).

There is great importance in remembering the tender mercies of the Lord. A record of these mercies can bring us strength in times of hardship, for in moments when we wonder if the Lord will help us through, we can look back at the times when He has done so before.

Daily recognizing His tender mercies and pausing to remember them will bring continual strength in our middle moments and will feed our soul like manna.

President Eyring taught, "Tonight, and tomorrow night, you might pray and ponder, asking the questions: Did God send a message that was just for me? Did I see His hand in my life or the lives of my children? I will do that. And then I will find a way to preserve that memory *for the day that I, and those that I love, will need to remember how much God loves us and how much we need Him*" ("O Remember, Remember," 69, emphasis added).

Do you have a place where you can keep a record of the daily tender mercies in your life?

The last time I read the Book of Mormon, I wanted to understand more about the tender nature of the Lord and how merciful He is toward us. I decided to try out Nephi's promise from the first chapter of the Book of Mormon, "But behold, I, Nephi, will show unto you that the tender mercies of the Lord are over all those whom he hath chosen, because of their faith, to make them mighty even unto the power of deliverance" (1 Nephi 1:20).

I decided to keep a journal as I read. In it, I kept track of the tender mercies and what they taught me about the character of the Lord, I wrote down what was required of me to recognize His mercies in my own life, and I listed the tender mercies that I experienced daily. The journal and the copy of the Book of Mormon in which I highlighted those lessons have become priceless possessions to me. Reading the Book of Mormon this way was an experience in my own middle moment that I won't ever forget. Here is what I discovered:

What Jesus Christ Does

Performs miracles	Makes weak things strong
Leads by the way	Hears prayers
Prepares a way	Sends comfort
Sends great blessings	Makes a desert a garden
Knows all things	Defends
Gives liberally	Offers a place of refuge

Provides a sanctuary	Will visit us
Increases joy	Sends angels
Remembers all	Delivers
Consoles in affliction	Allows men to prosper
Gives grace	Leads from captivity
Pours out His spirit	Asks what we desire
Fills hearts with joy	Speaks to us
Highly favors us	Softens hearts

Understanding the character of the Lord helped me to better understand the ways in which He can bless my life on a daily basis.

Do you need something from this list right now in your life?

What is it?

Perhaps you could circle a characteristic of the Lord from the list. Spend some time studying that characteristic in the scriptures, then watch more closely for His gentle hand in your life. Sometimes what we consider a coincidence is really a tender mercy from the Lord. As you see and recognize His gentle works of grace, His tender mercies in your life, write them down so that you will always remember them, so that you can look back on them from time to time.

With time you will discover that His promise is sure: Grace shall be as your day.

LESSON THREE

Recognize and Remember His Mercy

A Silver Lining

Several years ago, I was reading a children's novel to my daughter Grace. At the end of the first chapter, I read this little bit: "One thing I do know is, the more you worry, the more worries there are. . . . It's the worry you haven't even thought to worry about— that is the worry that should worry you the most. . . . How can you stop your worst worry from coming your way if you don't know what your worst worry could be?" (Lauren Child, *Clarice Bean, Don't Look Now,* 10–11).

That paragraph threw me for a loop! If there hadn't been anything to worry about before I started reading that children's novel, there certainly was now! Our family happened to be completely encompassed in a middle moment at the time, and I remember walking from Grace's room to my room wondering if there was something I should be worrying about that I hadn't even thought of yet.

I climbed into bed, and immediately my thoughts starting drifting off into worst-case scenarios. Does that ever happen to you? You can't help but list off everything that isn't going well and then adding two words to the end—*what if* . . . Before long you have added problems to your list that haven't even occurred yet and maybe never will.

It's the *What-If* syndrome.

Have you ever looked up the definition for the word *if?* It is defined by several phrases: "supposing, in the event that, despite the possibility, no matter whether . . ." Did you know that this very small word is mentioned fifteen times in the 122nd section of the Doctrine and Covenants? Following that word are fifteen worst-case scenarios—at least, that is how they feel to me. "If thou art accused . . . if thine enemies fall upon thee . . . with a drawn sword . . . [if] thine elder son, although but six years of age, shall cling to thy garments . . . [if] thou be dragged to prison . . . if thou shouldst be cast into the pit . . . if thou be cast into the deep; if the billowing surge conspire against thee . . . if the heavens gather blackness . . . if the very jaws of hell shall gape open the mouth wide after thee . . ." (D&C 122:6–7).

Lyman Wight describes the traumatic events in the Prophet Joseph Smith's life to which the verses in section 122 allude: "When passing his own house, [Joseph] was taken out of the waggon and permitted to go into the house, but not without a strong guard, and not permitted to speak with his family but in the presence of his guard; and his eldest son, Joseph, about six or eight years old, hanging to the tail of his coat, crying, Father, is the mob going to kill you? The guard said to him, 'You . . . little brat, go back; you will see your father no more'" (*Latter-day Saints' Millennial Star,* 21:539–40).

Those verses in Doctrine and Covenants 122 speak of a middle moment in Joseph Smith's life. He was unjustly imprisoned in Liberty Jail. The room that he shared with several other men was cold, dark, and cramped. It is not hard to imagine the Prophet, as he sat in those confined quarters, replaying that awful scene over and over again in his mind and then adding his own *what-ifs* to the list. During that moment, when it seemed there was no end in sight, I wonder if his prayers were filled with the one word we each tend to ask in troubled times—*why?*

There is a profound lesson to be found in the Lord's reply. *If that happens,* the Lord tells Joseph, *then know this,* "that all these things shall give thee experience, and shall be for thy good" (D&C 122:7).

Sometimes I can't help but wonder how those things could possibly be for anyone's good. Images fill my mind every time I read those verses—a son clinging to his father's shirt, prison doors closing, the heavens gathering with blackness. And I think, *Isn't every black cloud supposed to have a silver lining?* That yearning for the good hiding behind the darkness was expressed by poet John Milton, who penned these words:

O, welcome, pure-eyed Faith, white-handed Hope,
Thou hovering angel girt with golden wings, . . .
Was I deceived, or did a sable cloud
Turn forth her silver lining on the night?
("Comus")

I think about that sable cloud, filled with blackness, hovering and engulfing everything in its path with darkness. In times of worry, my heart knows that sable cloud. Perhaps you have felt it also a time or two, hanging over your world.

Hanging over your heart.

It hovered over Joseph's family—burdened, chased out, and stretched thin, with hearts worn through. As they clung to faith and held onto hope, where was the silver lining? Where was the good?

I am reminded of the next line in the scriptures: "The Son of Man hath descended below them all. Art thou greater than he?" (D&C 122:8). In that middle moment, Joseph was reminded to direct his thoughts to the Lord—to put aside his worry, the *what-ifs*, the doubt, and turn to Christ. It was through the

Atonement that Joseph would discover the light reaching through the darkness—the silver lining there.

In our moments of greatest worry, we must turn to the Savior. He knows how to get us through the middle moments because He has experienced them Himself. "And he shall go forth, suffering pains and afflictions and temptations of every kind; and this that the word might be fulfilled which saith he will take upon him the pains and the sicknesses of his people. And he will take upon him death, that he may loose the bands of death which bind his people; and he will take upon him their infirmities, that his bowels may be filled with mercy, according to the flesh, that he may know according to the flesh how to succor his people according to their infirmities" (Alma 7:11–12).

If, in the middle of this moment, you wonder whether anyone is aware of your situation, the answer is yes. The Lord is. He knows where you've been, and He knows where you need to go. He knows every *what-if* your mind has ever conjured up. He knows the worry that keeps you up at night. He sees you there holding on with white-handed hope, knuckles clinging and heart praying. He knows your faith. Most important, He knows how to help you through this because He experienced it Himself. He knows how to succor you. He will turn this to you for good. So, "Hold on thy way . . . *thy days are known* . . . therefore, fear not . . . for God shall be with you" (D&C 122:9; emphasis added).

> There is no anguish or sorrow or sadness in life that he has not suffered in our behalf and borne away upon his own valiant and compassionate shoulders.
>
> —Jeffrey R. Holland, *Christ and the New Covenant*, 224

Our days are known unto Him—all of them— the beginning and the end and every single day in between. The silver lining will come as we recognize that the Lord not only *knows* what we are going through, He has promised to journey with us and help

**People Who Have Turned
to the Savior
in Times of Need:**

Judges 7

1 Samuel 7

2 Kings 6

2 Chronicles 20

Matthew 11:28–30

Philippians 4:13

Philemon

1 Nephi 17

Helaman 5:12

D&C 19:23

D&C 68:6

Mosiah 23–24

us. Knowing that, we need never fear the sable cloud, no matter how threatening its darkness may appear.

You may wonder how to gain access to the Lord in these times of darkness. In the middle moments of this life, it is crucial that we learn of His Atonement and how it applies to each one of us and to the people we love. Elder Tad R. Callister has written, "Every attempt to reflect upon the Atonement, to study it, to embrace it, to express appreciation for it, however small or feeble it may be, will kindle the fires of faith and work its miracle" (*The Infinite Atonement*, 17).

How do we begin this sincere study? A good place to start is to search the scriptures for people who have received strength through the Atonement. Learning to understand how the Savior helped them in their time of need will help us to understand how He can help us in ours.

Sometimes the thought of a study of the Atonement may overwhelm us. If you feel overwhelmed, remember the counsel of Elder Callister about *"every attempt . . . however small or feeble . . ."* We may feel that our efforts are small and feeble, but the Lord will always bless a seeking heart.

A friend of ours experienced this blessing many years ago. He was sitting in sacrament meeting next to his young son. As he prepared to partake of the sacrament, he opened up his scriptures to the section in the Doctrine and Covenants where the sacramental prayers are found. He wanted to study the prayers as he reflected upon the Atonement quietly. Suddenly, his little boy reached out his tiny hand and grabbed the thin paper, ripping the whole page right out of the scriptures. After church the father came home and carefully taped the page back into place. Now, he says, every time he looks at that page in his scriptures, he is reminded that the times when we feel torn apart are the times we need the Atonement the most.

You might consider that father's effort as being small—his study of the Atonement probably lasted a very few minutes and was stopped short when his son ripped the page. However, even though his effort had been small, his fire of faith had been kindled. He learned a powerful lesson as he reflected on the Atonement, and he was strengthened. The lesson is true for each of us—the moments when we are torn apart, brokenhearted, and downtrodden truly are the moments when we need the Atonement the most.

If you are in a middle moment, if a dark cloud hangs over your heavy heart, if your mind is filled with worry, know this, "You cannot sink farther than . . . Jesus Christ can reach. I bear testimony that as long as there is one spark of the will . . . to reach, *he is there*" (Truman G. Madsen, *Christ and the Inner Life*, 14).

The silver lining turned forth from the sable cloud will come from Him.

Look for it, and it will be there.

LESSON FOUR

Rely on the Atonement

5

Continue to Minister

Have you ever had one of those moments when you are not sure if you can put one foot in front of the other? Maybe there's been a time when the trail has been going uphill for longer than you anticipated, or when the load you carry is too heavy for one person to bear alone.

How do we make it through those moments?

A promise from the scriptures has always brought me great comfort: "For he shall give his angels charge over thee, to keep thee in all thy ways. They shall bear thee up in their hands" (Psalm 91:11–12).

I believe angels are real. I know they are—because in moments of discouragement and doubt, when I haven't had the strength to put one foot in front of the other, the Lord has sent angels to bear me up. To strengthen me. To help lift the heavy load I could never have carried on my own.

I don't know what your circumstances are today. Perhaps you are in desperate need of heaven's help. If so, I pray the Lord will give His angels charge over you. But even more important, I pray that He will open your eyes to recognize the angels that He sends. For angels come in different shapes and sizes, and bearing up comes in ways we might not anticipate. What if the bearing up involves something that seems almost contrary to what we would expect in the middle of a trial? What if the bearing up requires something from us?

> "When we speak of those who are instruments in the hand of God, we are reminded that not all angels are from the other side of the veil. Some of them we walk with and talk with—here, now, every day. Some of them reside in our own neighborhoods."
>
> —Jeffrey R. Holland, "The Ministry of Angels," 30

"Trials give us the development of spirituality that we probably never would get if we didn't have the experience where the very jaws of hell gape open their mouth wide after us. Not only must we survive, but *we must develop the ability to have a concern for others while we are suffering.* It is a key element in our spiritual growth. As we lose our lives in the service of our fellowmen, we find ourselves" (Robert D. Hales, "Your Sorrow," 66; emphasis added). The advice here is that *sometimes we have to be the angel* even in the times when we are in need of the angel. Especially in those times.

In the third book of Nephi, the Savior describes how we can bear up others who are struggling. He asks that we do not cast them out from among us, but that we minister unto them and pray for them. "Unto such shall ye continue to minister," He pleads, "for ye know not but what they will return . . . and come unto me with full purpose of heart, and I shall heal them; and *ye shall be the means* of bringing salvation unto them" (3 Nephi 18:32; emphasis added).

I shall heal them.
Ye shall be the means.
Continue to minister.

Some of our most sacred moments in life will be those in which we continue to minister. In those moments, we live after the errand of angels—we become the means by which others come to Christ. In those moments, we find ourselves.

We might wonder, when we feel like we are waiting for our own angel, how we can be an angel for someone else. How can we be the means if we are in the midst of our own middle moment? How can we continue to minister? I learned a good lesson about this from Joseph Millett, an early member of the Church, who with his family was living in difficult circumstances. He wrote in his journal:

"One of my children came in and said that Brother Newton Hall's folks was out of bread, had none that day.

"I divided our flour in a sack to send up to Brother Hall. Just then Brother Hall came.

"Says I, 'Brother Hall, are you out of flour?'

"'Brother Millett, we have none.'

"'Well, Brother Hall, there is some in that sack. I have divided and was going to send it to you. Your children told mine that you was out.'

"Brother Hall began to cry. He said he had tried others, but could not get any. He went to the cedars and prayed to the Lord, and the Lord told him to go to Joseph Millett.

"'Well Brother Hall, you needn't bring this back. If the Lord sent you for it you don't owe me for it.'

My favorite part of this story is the line Joseph wrote in his journal after recording that experience: "You can't tell . . . how good it made me feel to know that the Lord knew there was such a person as Joseph Millett" ("Diary of Joseph Millett," holograph).

The lesson I love most in this story is that Joseph Millett was himself suffering through very, very difficult times. And yet, in the midst of his own middle moment, he continued to minister, and the Lord *knew* he was such a person as that.

I have had the opportunity in my lifetime to associate with people who continue to minister even in the middle moments of their lives. They have been the means of bringing many souls to Christ. They are people whom I admire and look up to. One of them is my daughter Megan.

There are many stories I could tell you about Megan's capacity to minister, but one of my favorites happened on a pioneer trek at Sixth Crossing in Wyoming.

When the pioneers were crossing the plains, some of the men went off to war, were called to serve missions, or passed away. The women were then left to pull the carts alone. In memory of this great sacrifice, many women who go on pioneer treks participate in what is called a women's pull.

In case you have never experienced a women's pull, let me explain to you how it works. At Sixth Crossing in Wyoming, the handcarts are stopped at the bottom of a steep hill, which climbs three-quarters of a mile up the mountainside. At this stopping point, the men are called out of the group, leaving the women and girls to pull the handcarts up the hill alone.

Just imagine a strenuous hike. Now imagine adding a handcart filled with buckets and water jugs. The summer temperature generally hovers around 95 degrees. There is no refuge from the heat. The sun bakes down on the dusty hill as you make your way up the steep incline.

I can remember the exhaustion of the moment, my muscles shaking, my lungs gasping for breath. I can remember looking up the hill at the first of the handcarts that were rounding the final bend and wishing that I were in their place. My daughter Meg was pulling that first cart; I saw her reach the top of the hill. I can remember focusing my eyes back down on the ground with an increased will to use the very last of my reserves to make it to the top.

And then, I can remember hearing the sound of pounding feet.

I will never forget looking up to see Megan and

the other girls who had pulled their cart ahead of us setting down their handcart and, without even stopping for a drink, turning and running back to those of us who were still pulling up the hill. They had already carried their burden, they were exhausted, and still they came running to help.

Isn't that what we do when we see someone in the midst of a middle moment that seems as if it might destroy them? We come running. In that instant, we become angels who help to bear heavy burdens, to bring comfort, and to encourage. As we set aside our own burdens for a time, we receive needed strength, compassion, and endurance. In blessing, we are blessed.

Annie Henrie captured a women's pull in a painting titled *All Is Well*. The painting is filled with women, young women, and baby girls. If you look closely, you see that some of the women and children are dressed completely in white, and you realize that the painting includes sisters from both sides of the veil. That painting became a favorite of mine after I participated in that women's pull at Sixth Crossing. It hangs above our front door as a reminder that in our family, no matter the situation, even if we carry a burden of our own, we come running.

President Spencer W. Kimball taught, "God does notice us, and he watches over us. But it is usually through another person that he meets our needs. Therefore, it is vital that we serve each other" ("The Abundant Life," 4).

> "Select just two or three individuals in your life who have been most influential, and ask yourself what they did specifically that was most helpful to you at the critical, important times of your life."
> —Spencer W. Kimball, "The Abundant Life," 5

As we reflect on the service given to us during the critical and important times in our own lives, perhaps it will better prepare us to serve others in their own critical and important times. As we live after the errand of angels, we too become such a person as

Joseph Millett was: a person the Lord can count on to continue to minister even in the midst of our own middle moments.

A person who will come running.

LESSON FIVE

Continue to Minister

6

God's Purpose

On a large acreage in the town of Concord, Massachusetts, sits an old two-story home in which Sophia and Nathaniel Hawthorne lived for a time. This old home has been carefully preserved. Even the windows are still intact. Last fall I had the opportunity to tour this home. I couldn't wait to reach the second story because the windowpane in the upstairs study was of particular interest to me.

It has been said that Sophia stood at this window and looked out on the scenery during a devastating middle moment in her life. After the tour guide finished explaining Sophia's experience to us, the tour moved on to the next room. But I stood at the window and pondered. The view from that window is breathtaking. Green lawns slope gently toward the banks of a river peacefully flowing under the shade of New England trees that reach up heavenward to blue sky. It is a scene that inspires reflection.

You might wonder how it is known that Sophia stood at this particular window and reflected on what was happening in her life. It is because she inscribed a message with the diamond of her wedding ring into the windowpane. It reads, "Man's accidents are God's purposes."

In that devastating middle moment, Sophia had learned an important truth: It is only as we align our hearts with the will of God that we begin to understand His purposes in the middle moments of our lives.

Elder Neal A. Maxwell taught: "There may be those who choose to debate the significance of whether or not an omnipotent God *gives* us a particular trial or simply *declines to remove it.* The outcome is obviously the same either way; God is willing for us to undergo that challenge. Yet He promises us that His grace is sufficient for us. (2 Corinthians 12:9; Ether 12:26–27.) He even indicates that some of the weaknesses and infirmities given to us can actually become a strength to us. It is in our weakness and extremity that God's power is fully felt. Only when, of ourselves, we are helpless is His help truly appreciated" (*All These Things Shall Give Thee Experience,* 31).

Once, when I was in the middle moment of a trial that had been ongoing for several months with no end in sight, my sister, Sara, called to ask if I was keeping a journal of the lessons I was learning. Then she gave me some words of advice that I wrote down because I wanted to never forget them: "Sometimes He refines us in ways we might not have wanted because He needs to use us in ways we might not have thought."

When she said that, it became crystal clear to me that I did not have an inkling of God's purpose for me. I knew that I was being refined in ways that I didn't want. But I felt that the place I was at was unnecessary, even a mistake. It hadn't occurred to me that there might be a purpose to what I was going through. In that moment I opened my heart to God. I wanted to understand His purpose.

It was as I opened my heart that the source of the trial no longer mattered. I still don't know whether it was an accident or not. But I do know this: from that day forward I did not journey alone. I felt Him there in the middle—guiding, encouraging, blessing. He gave me the needed strength to take the next step, and the next, and every one after. And after that trial ended, I realized that His purpose is to get us through whatever happens.

Here are two scriptures we can cling to in these moments:

"Great is his wisdom, marvelous are his ways, and the extent of his doings none can find out. *His purposes fail not,* neither are there any who can stay his hand" (D&C 76:2–3; emphasis added).

"*If God be for us, who can be against us? . . . Who shall separate us from the love of Christ?* shall tribulation, or distress, or persecution, or famine, or nakedness, or peril, or sword? . . . Nay, in all these things we are *more than conquerors* through him that loved us" (Romans 8:31, 35, 37; emphasis added).

From those two scriptures we learn two truths that can help build our trust in God: His purposes fail not, and nothing can separate us from His love.

Yes, sometimes life doesn't go the way we plan. There are times when we face a trial that seems to overwhelm us. When there is no end in sight, we might wonder if we will be forever held in that middle moment. We question if perhaps the Lord has forgotten us, if maybe things won't work out this time. We pray, and we fast, and we search desperately for the answers that never seem to come.

In the moments when we find ourselves wondering about His will and questioning His purpose for us perhaps we could remember a quote that hangs on the wall of my mother's bedroom:

When you can't see God's hand,
trust His heart.

Often our middle moments come from out of nowhere, when least expected. It is what we do when we encounter the unexpected that defines us. We could shrink, turn aside, curl up, and decide never to move forward again. And sometimes we do, just like King Hezekiah in the Old Testament, who turned his face to the wall and wept sore (see 2 Kings 20:2–3). But, in Hezekiah's case, after the weeping, something important took place. He turned to God. He prayed. And he came to know that God's heart was a heart he could trust. The prophet Isaiah told him, "Thus saith the Lord, . . . I have heard thy prayer, I have seen thy tears: behold, I will heal thee" (2 Kings 20:5–6). We too must come to know God's heart.

Here is what I know about God's heart.

His heart is full of wisdom
. . . for His words preserved on holy pages can bring
     comfort, direction, counsel, and guidance.
His heart is full of understanding
. . . for every silver lining turned forth from sable
     cloud comes from Him.

His heart is full of tenderness
. . . for He sends blessings from heaven and ministers
    with mercy.
His heart is full of hope
. . . for even if today the obstacle seems impossible
    to surmount, He has promised that tomorrow
    He will work wonders among you.
His heart is full of compassion
. . . for He sends angels who come running and
    continue to minister.
His is a heart we can trust
. . . because His purposes fail not, and nothing can
    separate us from His love.

This moment in the middle will not last forever. There will be an end, an answer, and a promise. All these things shall eventually work together for your good.

But right here and now, you have the privilege of journeying with the Lord.

Enjoy the journey, for I have found that we come to know Him best in the moments when we need Him most. Years from now, when you look back, you might discover that this moment, right here in the middle, was one of the most precious moments of your life.

Because it led your heart to His.

LESSON SIX

Trust God's Heart

Sources

Bednar, David A. "The Tender Mercies of the Lord." *Ensign,* May 2005, 99–102.

Callister, Tad R. *The Infinite Atonement.* 2000.

Child, Lauren. *Clarice Bean, Don't Look Now.* 2008.

Eyring, Henry B. "O Remember, Remember," *Ensign,* November 2007, 66–69.

Hales, Robert D. "Your Sorrow Shall Be Turned to Joy," *Ensign,* November 1983, 65–67.

Holland, Jeffrey R. *Christ and the New Covenant.* 1997.

———. "The Ministry of Angels." *Ensign,* November 2008, 29–31.

Kimball, Spencer W. "The Abundant Life." *Ensign,* July 1978, 3–7.

Madsen, Truman G. *Christ and the Inner Life.* 1978.